Todd Calls to a New Pal

By Cameron Macintosh

Todd is sad.
His best pal, Ben, left
for a new school.

Todd and Ben played ball,
rolled down big hills
and sang songs!

I miss Ben.

"You will get a new pal,"
said Dad.
"School is full of fun kids."

“Out of all the kids at school, **which** kid can I be pals with?” said Todd.

The next day,
Todd rested next
to a tall wall.

A kid was singing!

“You sing well!” called Todd.

Kat rolled up to the wall.

"I am Todd," said Todd.
"I love to sing, too."

"Will you sing with me
in the school hall?" said Kat.

"Yes!" called Todd.

The small hall was full of kids.

Todd and Kat sang two songs very well.

CHECKING FOR MEANING

1. Where does Dad suggest Todd could find a new pal? *(Literal)*
2. How does Todd meet Kat? *(Literal)*
3. How do Todd's feelings change from the beginning of the story to the end? *(Inferential)*

EXTENDING VOCABULARY

new	Read the word *new*. Do you have something that is new? What is a word that means the opposite of *new*?
full	What does it mean if something is *full*? If you replace the letter *f* with the letter *p*, what word can you make?
hall	Read the word *hall*. How many letters are in this word? How many sounds are there? What might you see performed in a hall?

MOVING BEYOND THE TEXT

1. Todd and Kat sang songs in the school hall. If you were to perform for other people, what would you do?
2. Where else might people sing? Is there a choir at your school? Have you ever been to a concert?
3. Sometimes it's easier to make friends if you have something in common. Why do you think this is?
4. Have you ever had to make a new friend? How did you do it?

SPEED SOUNDS

ull

all

PRACTICE WORDS

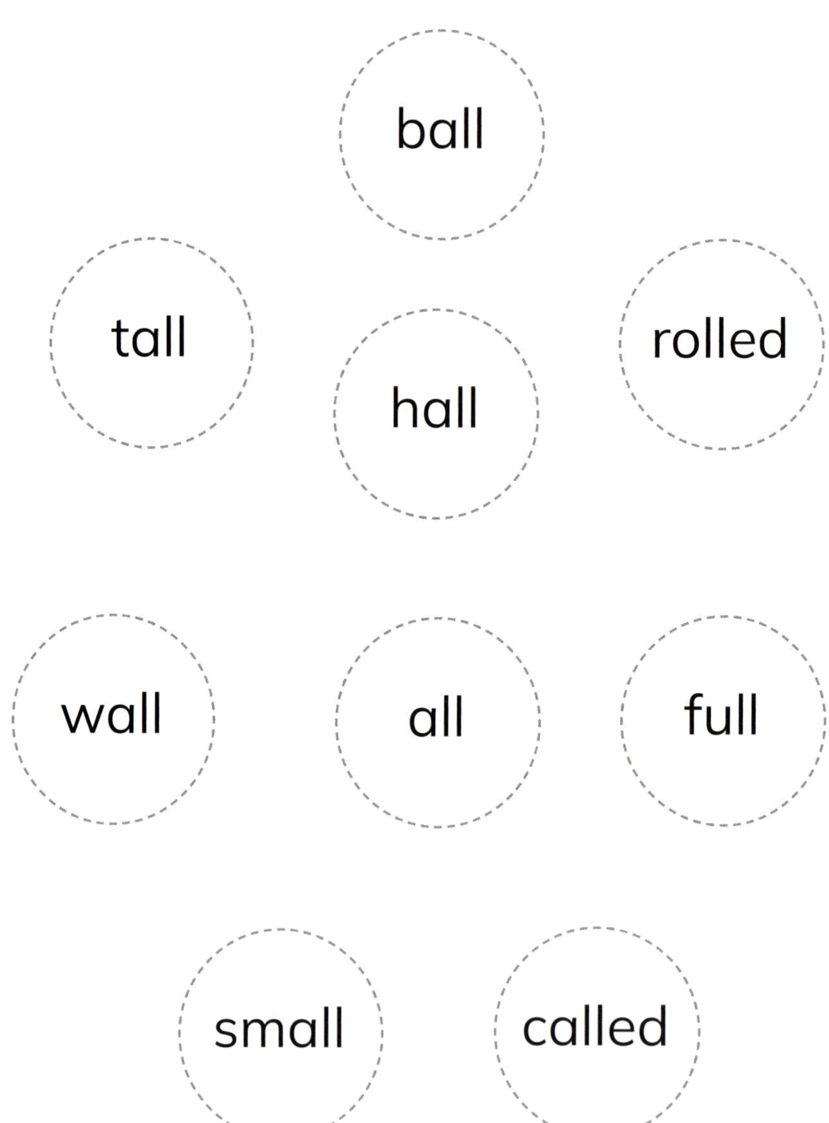